THE U.S. CONSTITUTION

BY MARCIA AMIDON LUSTED

Published by The Child's World®
1980 Lookout Drive • Mankato, MN 56003-1705
800-599-READ • www.childsworld.com

ACKNOWLEDGMENTS
The Child's World®: Mary Swensen, Publishing Director
Red Line Editorial: Editorial direction and production
The Design Lab: Design

Photographs ©: AS400 DB/Corbis, cover, 2, 8; Everett Historical/
Shutterstock Images, 5, 7; Shutterstock Images, 11; Carolyn
Kaster/AP Images, 13; Pool/Corbis, 15; Richard T. Nowitz/Corbis,
18; Bettmann/Corbis, 19; Andrea Izzotti/Shutterstock Images, 21

ISBN 9781503809079
LCCN 2015958461

Printed in the United States of America
PA02349

On the cover: Early American leaders met to
discuss and plan the Constitution in 1787.

TABLE OF CONTENTS

CHAPTER 1

CREATING A COUNTRY

In 1783, the United States was a new country. Americans had fought for independence from Britain. The war lasted for eight years. Both sides had fought bravely. In the end, the United States won its independence. Americans were free.

People celebrated the victory. Yet there was work to be done. The nation's founders needed to establish a government. They had fought against a British king. The founders did not want Americans to be ruled by a king. They needed to create a fairer government. They would make sure the government was not too powerful. They would try to preserve Americans' **liberty**.

During the war, the founders had written the Articles of Confederation. This document was the first U.S. constitution. It gave certain powers to the national government. These powers included signing treaties and coining money. The government could also direct the war

**During the Revolutionary War, the Continental
Army fought for freedom from British rule.**

effort. Most powers were left to the states. By 1781, all
13 states had **ratified** the document.

The Articles of Confederation helped unite the country.
But this document established only a weak government.
The government lacked many important powers. It could
not collect taxes. There was no money to pay the army.
During the war, the nation had borrowed money from other
countries. There was no way to pay back these debts. The

founders feared what might happen. Without a stronger government, the new nation might not survive.

The founders decided to write a new constitution. They called a **convention** in May 1787. Together, they began to write the document. More than 50 **delegates** worked through a long, hot summer. These delegates included Alexander Hamilton, Benjamin Franklin, and James Madison. The work was difficult. Some delegates did not want a stronger government. They thought it would take powers from the states. One state, Rhode Island, refused to send delegates. The other states agreed to work together.

George Washington was the president of the convention. Washington took this job seriously. He wore his military uniform to meetings. Washington rarely joined debates. His job was to keep the meetings orderly. The delegates valued his leadership. Later, Washington would become the first U.S. president.

A committee had decided on a process. The meetings would be secret. Delegates would speak honestly. They would debate many issues. When they reached a final decision, they would make a public announcement.

George Washington led the convention. Washington had
commanded colonial forces during the Revolutionary War.

The delegates had to decide on the roles of national and
state governments. They had to decide how much power
each state would have. The government would include a
congress. The congress would have **representatives** from
each state. Some states had larger populations than others.
Should each state have an equal amount of control? Or

A 1789 illustration showed a parade celebrating the ratification of the Constitution.

should larger states have more representatives? Delegates disagreed at first. But eventually they came to an agreement.

The document was finished on September 20, 1787. The Continental Congress voted to approve it. Next, it went to the state legislatures. Nine of the 13 states had to ratify it. This happened in 1788.

Soon, the government went to work. In March 1789, the U.S. Congress met for the first time. The next month, President George Washington took office. This new government could pass laws. Officials could collect taxes to pay debts. More states ratified the Constitution. By 1790, all states had ratified it.

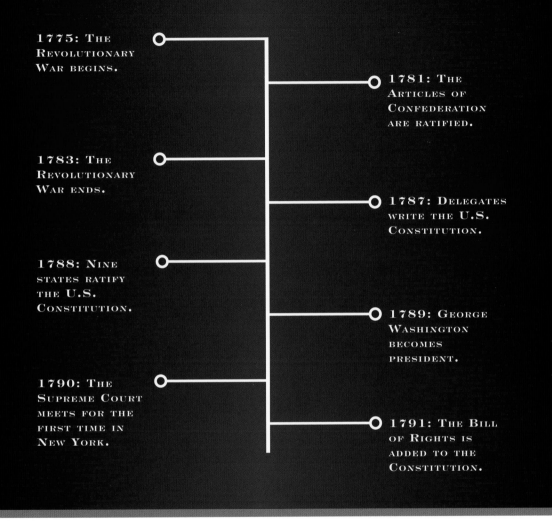

1775: THE REVOLUTIONARY WAR BEGINS.

1781: THE ARTICLES OF CONFEDERATION ARE RATIFIED.

1783: THE REVOLUTIONARY WAR ENDS.

1787: DELEGATES WRITE THE U.S. CONSTITUTION.

1788: NINE STATES RATIFY THE U.S. CONSTITUTION.

1789: GEORGE WASHINGTON BECOMES PRESIDENT.

1790: THE SUPREME COURT MEETS FOR THE FIRST TIME IN NEW YORK.

1791: THE BILL OF RIGHTS IS ADDED TO THE CONSTITUTION.

The new document wasn't perfect. But it was clearer than the Articles of Confederation. It also gave the government more powers. Officials needed these powers to unite the states. Over time, the nation would change. The Constitution would remain the law of the land.

CHAPTER 2

THE PREAMBLE AND ARTICLES

Why does a nation need a constitution? Some countries do not have one. But a constitution can help protect people's rights. It also explains how the government works.

The U.S. Constitution has three parts. The first part is called the Preamble. This part explains why the document was written. One reason was to create a "more perfect Union." The Constitution would bring the states together. Another reason was to defend the country. The United States would need to protect itself from other nations. The Constitution gave the government the power to declare war. A third reason was to protect people's liberty.

After the Preamble, there are seven articles. These include rules and procedures. They set out how the country is run. The articles describe the roles of each part of the government.

The Preamble to the Constitution is etched into the side
of the U.S. Courthouse in Boston, Massachusetts.

The articles divide the government into three main parts.
These parts are the legislative branch, the executive branch,
and the judicial branch. Different articles describe each
branch. Each branch has its own responsibilities.

Article 1 is about the legislative branch. This branch
makes laws. It includes the U.S. Congress. The Congress
has two houses, or parts. These are the Senate and the

House of Representatives. Representatives from each state are elected to each house.

The delegates had disagreed about the number of representatives. Some said all states should have the same number. Others said larger states should have more representatives. Eventually, the two sides compromised. Each state has two senators. In the House of Representatives, the number is based on state populations. Larger states have more representatives. Smaller states have fewer.

Article 2 is about the executive branch. This branch enforces the laws. It includes the president and the vice president. It also includes the president's Cabinet. Members of the Cabinet advise the president. Each member leads a federal department.

The president is the leader of the government. When Congress passes bills, the president can sign them into law or **veto** them. The president also commands the armed forces. The executive branch directs U.S. foreign relations. The president represents American interests in the world.

Article 3 is about the judicial branch. This branch is the court system. It interprets what laws mean. It includes the

In December 2015, President Barack Obama signed a
budget bill into law. Presidents can sign or veto bills.

Supreme Court and other federal courts. Judges apply
laws to specific cases. They can decide whether a law is
constitutional. The Constitution is the highest law of the
land. No other laws can violate it.

Each branch of government has a role. There is a system
of checks and balances. This system keeps each branch
from getting too powerful. One example involves laws.
The legislative branch makes laws. The president can veto
the laws. The judicial branch can **overturn** laws. These are

THE THREE BRANCHES OF GOVERNMENT

LEGISLATIVE BRANCH

Includes the Senate and House of Representatives

Can make laws, vote on presidential appointments, and declare war

EXECUTIVE BRANCH

Includes the president, vice president, and Cabinet

Can sign or veto bills, appoint federal judges, and command the armed forces

JUDICIAL BRANCH

Includes the Supreme Court and other federal courts

Can interpret laws and decide if laws are constitutional

In 2016, Supreme Court justices attended the
president's yearly State of the Union speech.

checks on legislative power. They help prevent Congress
from passing unfair laws. The founders limited politicians'
power. They wanted to protect citizens from unjust rulers
with too much power.

The first three articles are about the federal government.
Article 4 is about the states. Each state has to respect
other states' laws. The states can have their own courts.
Article 4 also tells how to add more states to the country.
In the 1780s, there were 13 states. Settlers would later

explore lands to the west. If Congress agreed, these lands could become states.

The last three articles explain how the Constitution works. Article 5 tells how to change it. Representatives can propose **amendments**. These are changes or additions to the document. These changes can then be ratified by states. If enough states ratify them, they become part of the Constitution.

IMPEACHMENT

Congress has the power to impeach certain officials. Impeachment is a formal accusation of a crime. The House of Representatives can choose to impeach the official. Then the Senate decides whether to remove the official from office. Two presidents, Andrew Johnson and Bill Clinton, have been impeached. No presidents have been removed from office.

Article 6 says that the Constitution is the highest law of the land. Government officials must swear to **uphold** it. All other laws must agree with it. If they do not, they are not valid. Article 7 explains how to ratify the Constitution.

The seven articles established a system of government. It is a system we still use today. Yet the Constitution has not stayed the same. Over the years, Americans have added 27 amendments. They make up the third part of the Constitution.

CHAPTER 3

AMENDMENTS

The Constitution established a new government. It explained how the government would work. But the founders knew that the nation would change. Americans would face new challenges. Opinions about the government could change, too. The Constitution needed to adjust to these changes.

OLDEST CONSTITUTION

The U.S. Constitution is more than 200 years old. It is the oldest national constitution still in use. Many states have their own constitutions. Some are also very old. The Massachusetts state constitution is the oldest. It is from 1780.

The articles do not change, but people can add amendments. Congress can propose new changes. State legislatures can propose amendments, too. They can officially propose the changes at a convention.

Proposing an amendment is the first step. Then it must be

Students visit the original document of the
Constitution in Washington, DC.

In 1972, President Richard Nixon signed an official document recognizing the 26th Amendment. This amendment allowed 18-year-old citizens to vote.

ratified. Three-fourths of the states need to vote for it. This process is difficult. Only amendments with a lot of support become law.

The first ten amendments are known as the Bill of Rights. They outline Americans' basic freedoms. These include freedom of speech and religion. The Bill of Rights was written in 1789. It officially became part of the Constitution in 1791. It helped persuade some states to support the Constitution. Delegates knew it would protect people's rights.

Later amendments are also important. The Constitution promised equality and liberty. Yet in the 1700s, not every person had equal rights. Women and black Americans could not vote. Slavery was allowed in some states. Slaves were forced to work for no pay. They were not considered U.S. citizens. Amendments gave rights to women and black Americans. The 13th Amendment officially ended slavery. In 1865, it banned people from owning slaves. The 14th Amendment was ratified in 1868. It said all people born or **naturalized** in the United States were citizens. That included former slaves. In 1870, the 15th Amendment gave black men the right to vote. Many of these men had been slaves. For the first time, they could participate in elections. Fifty years later, the 19th Amendment was ratified. It gave women the right to vote.

REPEAL

Many amendments protect Americans' rights. Others introduce new rules for government. Amendments can also repeal or cancel other amendments. In 1920, the 18th Amendment was ratified. It outlawed making or selling liquor. In 1933, the 21st Amendment repealed the 18th Amendment.

**The 22nd Amendment limited presidents to
two terms in the White House.**

Some amendments added new election rules. The 22nd Amendment limited the president's time in office. It said a president could serve no more than two **terms**. Other amendments controlled government powers. The 27th Amendment restricted pay raises for Congress. It was passed in 1992.

The Constitution helped create the American government. The amendments protect every American. People can still amend the Constitution today. They can make sure it continues to protect our rights.

amendments (uh-MEND-ments) Amendments are additions or changes to documents. There are 27 amendments to the U.S. Constitution.

congress (CON-gress) A congress is a group of people elected to make laws. The United States has a congress with two parts, or houses.

constitutional (kon-sti-TOO-shun-ul) When something is constitutional, it agrees with the U.S. Constitution. The Supreme Court makes sure laws are constitutional.

convention (kun-VEN-shun) A convention is a formal meeting. Amendments to the Constitution can be proposed at a national convention.

delegates (DEL-i-gits) Delegates are people who represent a place or group. Delegates from the different states planned the Constitution.

liberty (LIB-er-tee) Liberty is freedom from outside control. Many of the amendments protect Americans' liberty.

naturalized (NACH-er-uh-lized) When people are naturalized, they become citizens of a nation. The U.S. government decides when people from other countries can be naturalized.

overturn (oh-ver-TURN) To overturn a law is to change or reverse it. The Supreme Court can overturn laws and court decisions based on the Constitution.

ratified (RA-ti-fide) When something is ratified, it has been signed and given formal approval. The states ratified the Constitution.

repeal (ri-PEEL) To repeal is to cancel or withdraw. An amendment can repeal another amendment.

representatives (rep-ri-ZEN-tuh-tivz) Representatives are people who can represent or speak for others. Government representatives might support laws to help their community.

terms (TURMZ) Terms are periods of time that politicians serve in office. Presidents serve four-year terms.

uphold (up-HOLD) To uphold is to support. U.S. officials must uphold the Constitution.

veto (VEE-toh) To veto a bill is to prevent or delay it from becoming law. Presidents have the power to veto bills.

TO LEARN MORE

IN THE LIBRARY

Furi-Perry, Ursula. *Constitutional Law for Kids: Discovering the Rights and Privileges Granted by the U.S. Constitution.* Chicago, IL: American Bar Association, 2013.

Sobel, Syl. *The U.S. Constitution and You.* Hauppauge, NY: Barron's, 2012.

Taylor-Butler, Christine. *The Constitution of the United States.* New York: Children's Press, 2008.

ON THE WEB

Visit our Web site for links about
the U.S. Constitution: **childsworld.com/links**

Note to Parents, Teachers, and Librarians: We routinely verify our Web links to make sure they are safe and active sites. So encourage your readers to check them out!

INDEX

ABOUT THE AUTHOR

Marcia Amidon Lusted has written more than 120 books
and 500 magazine articles for kids. She has also seen the real
Constitution in Washington, DC.